Fraction Action

written and illustrated by

Loreen Leedy

Holiday House • New York

Name a fraction between 4 and 5.

$4\frac{1}{2}$ $4\frac{2}{3}$ $4\frac{5}{6}$ $4\frac{99}{100}$

$4\frac{1}{63}$

For REBECCA

Thanks to Mrs. Mills
and her first-grade class,
Community Park School, Princeton, New Jersey

Library of Congress Cataloging-in-Publication Data
Leedy, Loreen.
    Fraction action / written and illustrated by Loreen Leedy. —1st
ed.
        p.   cm.
    Summary: Miss Prime and her animal students explore fractions by
finding many examples in the world around them.
    ISBN 0-8234-1109-5
    1. Fractions—Juvenile literature. [1. Fractions.] I. Title.
QA117.L44   1994   93-22800   CIP   AC
513.2'6—dc20
    ISBN 0-8234-1244-X (pbk.)

Contents

FrAcTioN AcTioN

One morning, Miss Prime turned off all the lights in the classroom.

Okay, everybody, watch the screen, and you'll see how to draw a fraction.

Start with a WHOLE shape.

Then make it into two equal parts.

Each part is called ONE HALF.

4

7

One Saturday at about noon, Sadie heard a loud knock at the door.

19

What fractions were used to make lunch? (Hint: there were 3 different fractions.) See page 32.

Lemonade For Sale

25

Tally subtracted three fourths $(\frac{3}{4})$ from the original price. If he subtracted another fourth $(\frac{1}{4})$, how much would he charge? The answer is on page 32.

Teachers Test

Miss Prime tapped her desk with a ruler.

Attention everyone! Today we're having a test on fractions.

Oh no!

Awooo!

This test will be a little different, because *you* will give *me* the problems to solve.

We will?

If I say the right answer, I get one point.

Who wants to start?

If I say the wrong answer and you catch me, the class gets a point.

Answers

page 10: The smallest fraction is ONE FOURTH.

$\frac{1}{2}$ $\frac{1}{3}$ $\frac{1}{4}$

page 15: There were 30 marbles in the whole set.

page 21: The fractions used to make lunch were:

ONE HALF ($\frac{1}{2}$), to slice the oranges

ONE FOURTH ($\frac{1}{4}$), to cut the watermelon

ONE FIFTH ($\frac{1}{5}$), to divide the fruit salad

page 27: If Tally subtracted another ONE FOURTH ($\frac{1}{4}$) from the original price, he would be charging zero.

page 31: Ginger is ONE FIFTH ($\frac{1}{5}$) of the set of Miss Prime's students.